FRED RAMEN

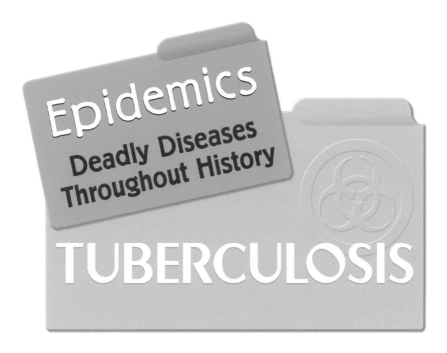

Epidemics
Deadly Diseases
Throughout History

TUBERCULOSIS

The Rosen Publishing Group, Inc.
New York

For my mother and father

Published in 2001 by The Rosen Publishing Group, Inc.
29 East 21st Street, New York, NY 10010

Library of Congress Cataloging-in-Publication Data

Ramen, Fred.
    Tuberculosis / By Fred Ramen. — 1st ed.
        p.   cm. — (Epidemics!)
Includes bibliographical references (p.   ) and index.
    ISBN 0-8239-3349-0 (library binding)
    1. Tuberculosis—History—Juvenile literature. [1. Tuberculosis. 2. Diseases.] I. Title. II. Series.
    RC310 .R35 2000
    616.9'95'009—dc21

                                                            00-009965

Cover Image: Light micrograph of a tuberculosis infection (pink) in a lymph node.

Manufactured in the United States of America

CONTENTS

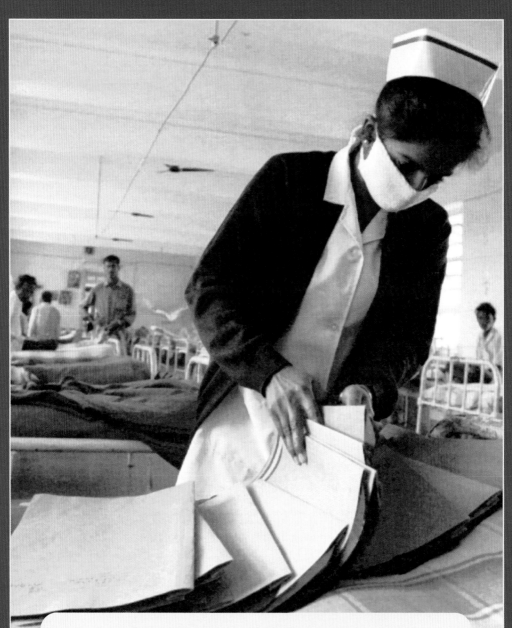

Although tuberculosis was considered curable for many years, new drug-resistant strains have recently appeared.

INTRODUCTION

On November 7, 1962, Eleanor Roosevelt died in New York City. In the course of her seventy-eight years, she had been an outstanding activist on behalf of the rights of the poor, minorities, and women. She remains revered as the greatest first lady in United States history because she worked hard not only to further many of the policies of her husband, President Franklin Delano Roosevelt, but also publicly fought for policies with which he disagreed (but about which she felt very strongly). Because the president suffered from polio—a disease that attacks the nervous system—which had left him paralyzed from the waist down, Eleanor frequently toured the nation, reporting back to him on the various conditions in which people lived.

After Franklin's death in 1945, Eleanor became a delegate to the United Nations, where she helped to write the Universal Declaration on Human Rights. She remained an internationally respected figure, meeting with many of the most important world leaders of the time until the day she died. By all accounts, her life was an active and rewarding one. But she was struck down by a disease that is still known for slowly sapping the life from even its most hearty victims, often leaving them helplessly coughing up blood from rotting lungs. It's a disease that can kill quickly, within a year or two, or hide within the body for decades before it causes death. It is the disease called tuberculosis.

Eleanor Roosevelt had contracted tuberculosis, which is often referred to as TB, as a young woman while visiting France. She apparently recovered from this early infection and went on to lead an extremely active life. But the disease remained hidden in her body and reemerged in her old age. Eleanor Roosevelt died of a disease she had caught almost fifty years earlier.

Eleanor Roosevelt's life illustrates many of the unusual and frustrating elements of tuberculosis, a disease that many believe has killed more people throughout history than any other. She was born when TB was still a common infection and the leading cause of death in America and much of Europe. She lived through the period of exciting discoveries about this mysterious

Eleanor Roosevelt (center) contracted tuberculosis as a young woman and died of it many years later. In the photo above, she is visiting the Hadassah's Children's TB Hospital in Jerusalem.

killer, including the discovery of the "miracle drugs" that finally made TB curable. Yet in the end, these miracle drugs could not help her; tuberculosis had the final victory. Today, the world faces a similar crisis, as new strains of the disease emerge that cannot be killed by current drugs.

Disease Throughout History

Deadly diseases have long played a crucial role in history. In 430 BC, Athens, the richest and most advanced of the Greek city-states and master of an empire that embraced much of the Greek world, seemed assured of victory against its aggressive neighbor, Sparta, in a war that had begun the year before. But two successive epidemics of a new plague so decimated the population of Athens that twenty years later, still not recovered from the effects, the great city surrendered to Sparta.

Similarly, the Roman Empire, already suffering from civil wars and barbarian invasions, was unable to cope with several plagues at the end of the fourth century. Soon, the glory that was Rome passed away.

Deciding the outcome of wars is not the only way in which deadly diseases have influenced world history. During the Middle Ages, the Black Death (or bubonic plague) killed between a third and a half of the population of Europe and caused enormous changes in European society. With so many dead, peasants found that their labor was in demand in the cities, so rather than remaining bound to the land, they were able to seek a better life. The cities, which were always struck harder by disease than the countryside, had an endless need for people, from craftsmen to unskilled laborers. People flocked to them. In this new urban life, art and education flourished with the influx of energy and excitement; people began to rediscover knowledge lost since Roman times and devise their own theories as to how the world worked. The period known as the Renaissance owes much to the horrors of the Black Death.

Humans have always struggled against infectious diseases—diseases that can be "caught." For most of history, though, people did not understand how diseases spread. One problem was that the cause of a disease was not always obvious. For example, tuberculosis often killed a person years after they had first become infected. Another problem was that two very different diseases may have the same symptoms, or the same disease may cause different symptoms in different people. For these reasons, diseases have been very difficult to understand throughout most of human history.

Gradually, as science advanced, people began to gain insight into the causes of many different diseases. It became clear that several diseases could be prevented simply by having good food (and enough of it), clean water, and proper sanitation. Unfortunately, these simple living standards were not available to most people. And even in communities where these conditions were met, plagues and epidemics could still mysteriously appear, infecting and killing large numbers of people.

With the invention of the microscope, humans were finally able to see the microorganisms that cause infectious diseases. Many diseases are caused by microorganisms called *bacteria*. By the end of the nineteenth century, scientists had observed many different kinds of bacteria through their microscopes, and identified many of those that cause disease in humans and animals. Vaccines were developed to protect people from several infectious diseases. By the middle of the twentieth century, plagues no longer troubled the rich nations of the world.

But nature is infinitely more resourceful than human ingenuity. New plagues appeared caused by viruses rather than bacteria: AIDS, a disease that destroys the body's ability to fight off infection, is the best known. It has already killed millions throughout the world. Terrifying new viral infections emerged, like Ebola, a very contagious tropical disease that causes the body to literally drown in its own blood. Suddenly, people began to talk about deadly epidemics again, as if they were something new.

But they were not new. In fact, tuberculosis, whose cure was one of the greatest medical stories of the twentieth century, would return at that century's close to again threaten people everywhere. And when teamed with a new infection, AIDS, it would prove to be even more deadly than before.

1

THE WHITE PLAGUE

Tuberculosis is an infectious disease that comes in numerous different forms. Each form of TB attacks a different part of the body, from the bones to the spine to the intestines. A particularly deadly form of the disease, military tuberculosis, causes the disease to spreads into the bloodstream, which carries it throughout the body. The most familiar form of tuberculosis, however, is pulmonary TB—tuberculosis of the lungs.

Tuberculosis attacks whatever area of the body it invades, eating away at it and leaving gaping holes in flesh and bone. It can cause the bones of the spine to weaken and collapse, leaving the infected person with a permanently hunched back. In the lungs, it feeds on

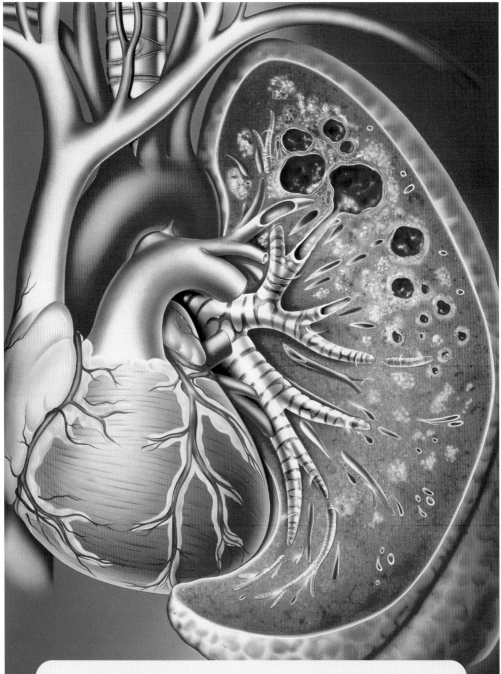

*Pulmonary tuberculosis, the most familiar form of
the disease, eats away at the delicate tissues of the lungs.*

the delicate tissues that take oxygen from the air and filter it into the blood. The area grows cheesy and fills with pus. As more and more of the lungs are destroyed, the infected person becomes weaker and weaker. He or she has trouble breathing, coughs constantly, suffers from high fever and night sweats, and loses his or her appetite. Eventually the tuberculosis will eat into one of the many small blood vessels that run throughout the lungs, and the infected person will have the disease's most terrifying symptom: the coughing up of blood. If the disease continues unchecked, it may eat into one of the arteries—the major blood vessels that carry blood away from the heart—and rupture it, causing a hemorrhage, or heavy, uncontrolled internal bleeding. This is usually the cause of death in people who suffer from TB. Even without a fatal hemorrhage, the infected person will continue to become weaker and weaker, until he or she eventually dies. This gradual wasting away was the reason the disease was commonly known as *consumption*.

Although tuberculosis has a long history throughout the world, it was particularly common in Europe and America during the eighteenth and nineteenth centuries. During that time, TB was the leading cause of death in all age groups and remained so even during the early twentieth century. The rapid growth of cities in Europe and America during this period caused many people to live in close proximity to each other, often in dirty and cramped conditions. Like any airborne disease, TB spreads much faster when people are gathered together in crowds. Tuberculosis became known as the White Plague, to differentiate it from the other great plague of European history, the Black Death of the fourteenth century.

Tuberculosis left a deep impression on society that has not faded even to this day. It was common for several generations of a family to become infected, or even for many members within one household—mother, father, brothers, and sisters— to die from the disease.

Some idea of how common and horrifying tuberculosis was in the nineteenth century can be found in the literature, art, and music of the time. Many novels and plays of the period have at least one character who has the disease. Often this person is either a mother (like in Charles Dickens' famous novel *Oliver Twist*) or a young hero or heroine who becomes infected and is prevented from living "happily ever after." Two of the most famous heroines in opera, Violetta (in Verdi's *La Traviata*) and Mimi (in Puccini's *La Boheme*) suffer from tuberculosis, leaving behind mourning lovers who have realized too late how much the dying person meant to them. Indeed, the most tragic aspect of tuberculosis

Mimi, the tragic heroine of Puccini's opera La Boheme, *died of tuberculosis.*

2000 BC
References to the disease in India.

3000 BC
Tuberculosis infects the people of Egypt.

496 AD
King Clovis of France begins custom of touching people to cure them of scrofula.

700
Mummies of people in Peru show signs of tuberculosis infection.

was that it killed many people in what would have been the prime of their lives, sapping them of their strength and making it impossible for them to enjoy their youth.

Tuberculosis was also associated with artistic genius, because so many great writers, poets and musicians died of it. This included people like Charlotte Brontë, author of *Jane Eyre*; Robert Louis Stevenson, author of *Treasure Island*; Anton Chekhov, the great Russian playwright and short story writer; Frederic Chopin, the great pianist and composer; John Keats, the English poet; and

1660
John Bunyan calls tuberculosis "the Captain of the men of Death."

1821
John Keats dies of tuberculosis.

1882
Dr. Robert Koch discovers tuberculosis bacteria.

1859
First tuberculosis sanatorium founded in Poland.

1889
Koch creates tuberculin.

(continued)

George Orwell, the author of *1984*. Although at the time it was thought that somehow artists were more susceptible to the disease because of heredity, or that being an artist somehow made you more likely to catch it, it seems more likely that the unhealthy living conditions that many artists were forced to accept (because they were poor) is the real explanation. Still, the image of the solitary artist or writer, gaunt and thin, eyes burning with feverish inspiration—all symptoms of tuberculosis—became a popular myth and survives in some form to the present day.

1921
Creation of the BCG vaccine.

1943
Selman Waksman discovers streptomycin.

1947
Domagk introduces Conteben.

1933
Gerhard Domagk introduces Prontosil.

1943
PAS synthesized by Jorgen Lehmann.

Everywhere a person looked during the nineteenth century, he or she could find evidence of tuberculosis. In American history, figures as diverse as Alexander Stephens, vice president of the Confederacy, and John "Doc" Holliday, the famous gunslinger, suffered from the disease. Almost any event in history during those years had some connection to the White Plague, from its inevitable increase following a war (when young men were crammed together in army barracks, greatly facilitating the spread of the disease) to the famous mutiny, or rebellion, on the British ship *Bounty*. The sailors

1962
Eleanor Roosevelt dies.

1985
Tuberculosis increases in the United States for the first time in over thirty years.

1990
Strain W emerges in New York. MDR tuberculosis cases become more common.

1982
AIDS first diagnosed in America.

1986
Relationship between tuberculosis and AIDS first described.

who seized the *Bounty* from the legendary Captain Bligh founded a new home on remote Pitcairn Island in the South Pacific. Years later, the descendants of those sailors were convinced to move to the island of Tahiti. There they encountered tuberculosis for the first time; although they returned to Pitcairn, the disease came with them, reducing their population from eighty-six to seventeen in less than a year.

Tuberculosis killed the young and the old. It killed slowly, over a period of many years, often not even producing any symptoms until the end. It also killed

The English poet John Keats was born in 1795. In his boyhood he was an excellent student and an active athlete who enjoyed sports, including boxing. When he was fourteen, though, his mother died of tuberculosis. Keats nursed her during her final days and may well have caught the disease from her.

After his mother's death, Keats decided to study medicine. In 1816, at the age of twenty-one, he became licensed to practice medicine. However, he was already becoming more interested in poetry than medicine, and he never actually became a physician.

In 1818, Keats began to display the first symptoms of tuberculosis. His health suffered, but he continued to work; in 1819, he produced some of his greatest poems.

In 1820 he began to cough up blood. With his medical training, he knew that this was a death sentence. The disease's progress was rapid, and Keats soon became extremely weak. He took a number of sea voyages and, at the urging of his friend, the poet Percy Bysshe Shelley, decided to go to Italy, where the climate was believed to help tuberculosis patients. He was severely ill throughout the voyage, coughing up blood frequently.

Keats only lived for three months once he arrived in Italy, dying in Rome on February 21, 1821. It took just over a year from the time his first major symptom appeared for tuberculosis to kill him, cutting short the life of a man some consider to be the greatest English poet since Shakespeare. Keats' story is tragic not only for the speed of his illness, but because his fate was a common one for generations of young people throughout the nineteenth century.

swiftly, striking some of its victims down in a period of a few years or even months. There was no cure and almost no way to treat the disease to stop its growth. It was a terror so common that it became a part of ordinary life. As the nineteenth century drew to a close, many scientists and doctors were dedicating their lives to finding a cure for the disease. It would take over fifty years for them to succeed.

2

TUBERCULOSIS IN HISTORY

Tuberculosis may be as old as human history. It is almost certainly older than civilization. The skeleton of an Egyptian girl from about 3000 BC shows clear signs of the effects of tuberculosis on her bones, resulting in the characteristic hunched back. In India, hymns were consecrated as a cure for the disease as early as 2000 BC. Tuberculosis was already infecting people in the Americas by 2000 BC, 3,500 years before Columbus crossed the Atlantic.

Tuberculosis is caused by a type of bacteria that lives in the soil. It spreads to humans in many ways when they breathe dusty air in which the bacterium lives, breathe the air that is coughed out by an infected person, or drink the milk of a cow that has been infected with the disease.

In ancient times, long before humans began to live in cities, the disease may have already begun infecting people, but because the groups of these early humans were so small and far apart, the disease could not reach epidemic proportions. Instead, the disease would tend to die out as soon as it had killed most of one group of people. Once all of the infected people were dead, there was no one left to continue spreading the disease. But when humans began to settle down and grow crops and build towns, villages, and cities, contact between large groups of people became common enough for the disease to continue spreading from population to population before it died out. The tuberculosis epidemic—which lasted until about fifty years ago—had begun.

All around the globe, the most common name for the pulmonary form of TB has been *consumption* because of the way people who have the disease waste away, as if being consumed or eaten from the inside. (The name was proven accurate when medical science grew advanced enough to see the actual effects of the disease on the body, for tuberculosis does indeed eat away at the body's organs and bones.) The ancient inhabitants of India called it *yakshma*; the ancient Hebrews called it *schanhepeth*, and the Book of Deuteronomy warned that if the Israelites did not follow God's commands, he would smite them with "the consumption."

The ancient Greeks were also familiar with tuberculosis, which they called *phthisis*, a name which continued to be used for the disease even in the nineteenth century, and which derives either from the Greek word meaning "to spit" (referring to the coughing or spitting up of blood in patients with pulmonary tuberculosis) or from the word meaning "to consume." The great Greek physician Hippocrates, who lived from around 460 BC to around 377 BC and is known as the father of medicine, described tuberculosis so clearly that his description of the disease is essentially the same one used to diagnose it today.

Galen (131–199 AD) was a Greek physician who theorized that tuberculosis was an infectious disease.

Another Greek physician, Galen, who lived in the Roman Empire from about 131 to 199 AD, also described tuberculosis. He believed that the disease was infectious and thought that the best treatment was fresh milk, open air, a dry climate, living at a high altitude,

One type of tuberculosis that was fairly common during the Middle Ages was *scrofula*, a condition where the neck is infected with tuberculosis, causing it to swell up without becoming painful. At the time, a tradition grew that kings, because they were thought to be chosen by God to lead their countries, had the power to heal sick people by touching them, just as it was believed Jesus had done. Scrofula was particularly singled out for this treatment and became known as the "King's Evil." The French king Louis XIV was said to have touched 2,500 people; Charles II of England was said to have touched 92,000 people between 1662 and 1682. The last English monarch to follow this practice was Queen Anne, who ruled England from 1702 to 1714. Among her "patients" was the famous Dr. Samuel Johnson, who suffered from scrofula as a young boy and was touched by the Queen in 1712. This did not seem to have any effect, as several years later he had an operation to drain the swellings on his neck and was eventually cured of the disease.

and sea voyages. It would take 1,800 years to discover any better treatment, and during that time much of his wisdom would be lost.

During the Middle Ages, tuberculosis became less common. This may be due to the rise of a disease known as leprosy. Leprosy has many symptoms in common with tuberculosis. For example, it can take a long time for a person who is infected to show symptoms of the disease. But unlike tuberculosis, leprosy can cause the extremities—fingers, toes, even the nose—to waste away and fall off.

The reason why leprosy cut down on the number of cases of tuberculosis is that people who have been infected with leprosy become immune to tuberculosis. This is because the bacteria that cause each disease are very similar. And since leprosy was much more common in Europe during the Middle Ages, fewer people caught tuberculosis.

Another reason there may have been fewer cases of tuberculosis reported was because it may have been misdiagnosed. A type of tuberculosis called *lupus vulgaris* infected the bones of the face, causing it to eventually cave in around the nose. This may have frequently been mistaken for leprosy.

As the cities of Europe grew larger, tuberculosis became more common, especially in its more vicious and deadly forms. True consumption, rather than scrofula or other secondary forms, reemerged. King Louis XIII of France died of the disease in 1643; tuberculosis also claimed the life of the great philosopher Spinoza in 1677. During the 1600s, TB was infecting people in London at nearly twice the rate that AIDS infects people in the United States today. Tuberculosis was more common than almost any other killer infection, and more feared than any other disease, with the possible exception of the Black Death,

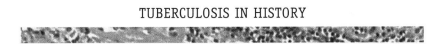

which had its last outbreak in England in the 1660s. So terrifying was TB that the English religious writer John Bunyan called the disease "the Captain of the men of Death."

The Captain would move on to become the deadliest disease in Europe. Eventually though, scientists would discover new tools to combat him and similar "men of death."

3

THE HUNT FOR THE KILLER

To understand why it took so long to discover a cure for tuberculosis, we must first learn more about the disease and the many peculiar characteristics which kept its true nature hidden from science for centuries.

Tuberculosis is caused by bacteria called *mycobacterium tuberculosis*. Bacteria are microscopic organisms. Many bacteria live on dead animals and plants and help cause the process known as decomposition or rotting; others live inside living animals and plants. Many are relatively harmless, and a few are even helpful, such as the bacteria that live inside the human intestine and help digest some foods. But some bacteria have the ability to cause disease in animals and plants—and of these, *mycobacterium tuberculosis* is one of the worst.

The tuberculosis bacterium is one of the hardiest kinds of bacteria in the world. It can survive in the soil for months without nourishment. Its rod-like shape is enclosed in a tough capsule of material that is difficult to destroy. This is one of the reasons that tuberculosis is so diffi-cult to get rid of: nor-mally, the body's natural defenses can destroy invading germs by using specialized cells that surround and consume them. But the tough outer shell, or "capsule," of the tuberculosis bac-terium cannot bede-stroyed by these defenses, allowing it to grow with little resistance.

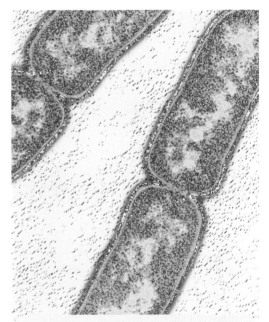

Tuberculosis is caused by rod-shaped bacteria called mycobacterium tuberculosis.

Even so, the tubercu-losis bacterium does not grow particularly rapidly. Indeed, one of the chal-lenges to scientists was finding a way to make it grow outside of the body so it could be studied. The slow way in which the disease spreads is the reason that people who come down with tuberculosis will sometimes not show any symptoms for many years, and why others who show symptoms can live for a long time with the disease.

Only 5 to 7 percent of people who come in contact with the bacteria will develop the disease. In other people, the body's defenses form a hard wall around the invading bacteria. These tiny spots are called *tubercles* and give the disease its name. In most people, walling the bacterium up will keep it from spreading. However, in others this isn't enough, especially if they have repeated contact with the disease. In these people, the infection continues to grow, killing the cells it comes in contact with; the

Because tuberculosis often affected entire families (like the Brontë family, shown here), it was believed the disease was hereditary.

tubercles expand and merge together, eventually causing holes called lesions in the affected organs. As mentioned earlier, in the lungs this often results in the rupture of a blood vessel, which can kill a person.

The story of the Brontë family, three of whom—the sisters Charlotte, Emily, and Anne—became famous writers, is noteworthy not only because it illustrates how tuberculosis ravaged entire families, but as an insight into why many people believed the disease was hereditary.

Patrick Brontë, the father, was a Methodist minister who is believed to have suffered from tuberculosis for most of his life. His wife, Maria, died in 1820 after giving birth to their youngest daughter, Anne. Although there are questions as to the cause of her death, many facts point to tuberculosis.

In 1825, one of the Brontë's children, also named Maria, died at the age of twelve from tuberculosis. Within a month, her sister, Elizabeth, died from it as well. She was eleven years old.

The family suffered no more from the dreaded illness until 1848, when both Emily Brontë and the only son in the family, Bramwell, died of it within three months of each other. Two weeks after Emily's death, Anne was diagnosed with tuberculosis, too. She died in 1849. Charlotte Brontë survived until 1855, when she died of a wasting disease that most probably was tuberculosis. Their father lived to be eighty-five years old.

Extreme experiences like those the Brontë family endured were not uncommon at the time. Children of parents with tuberculosis often died of the disease themselves. Today we know that this was because close contact among family members promotes the spread of the tuberculosis bacteria; but until the bacterium was discovered, no one could prove that tuberculosis was infectious. Thus, cases like that of the Brontës helped reinforce the idea that the disease was inherited.

Because it can take so long for the disease to develop, for a long time some people thought that tuberculosis was not infectious, but hereditary, or passed down genetically from parent to child. Some families had many more people with the disease than other families; today we know that this was because families living with an infected person have a much greater risk of catching the disease. It does seem, however, that some people inherit a greater susceptibility to tuberculosis. Even so, these people must have contact with TB bacteria in order to contract the disease.

Another reason that it took so long to identify the cause of tuberculosis is that there are several different ways that the disease can be caught. For example, it is possible to catch it from some animals and, as mentioned earlier, the most common way of doing so is to drink the milk of a cow infected with bovine, or cow-related, tuberculosis. (TB was fairly common among cattle until the development of an effective vaccine and widespread pasteurization of milk made it exceptionally rare in Europe and America.) But if you are around a person who is sick with TB, or if the air around you is dusty and filled with the bacteria, you can catch tuberculosis just by breathing in.

The final reason that it took so long to find the cause of tuberculosis is that for most of human history, people thought that it was impossible that something too small to see could harm a person. Only after the development of the microscope in the late seventeenth century was it possible to see these tiny bacteria, and it still took over a century to finally prove that some of them caused diseases.

As late as the 1880s, many reputable scientists thought that tuberculosis was an inherited disease. One man—Robert Koch—believed otherwise, however, and spent much of his life in pursuit of the cause and cure of the disease.

Koch was born in Germany in 1843. He was an extremely intelligent man, and by the age of twenty-three he became a medical doctor. In 1876, he proved that the sheep disease anthrax was caused by a particular bacterium—an amazing achievement, given the technology of the day. He next

The development of the microscope enabled scientists to see bacteria.

In 1882, a German scientist, Dr. Robert Koch,
identified the bacterium that causes tuberculosis.

In the course of his research into the cause of tuberculosis, Koch perfected the method known as "pure culture," whereby a certain type of bacteria was grown without contamination from any other bacteria. This made it possible to test which bacteria caused which disease.

At about this time, Koch formulated his four postulates for determining which microorganism causes a particular disease. They are:

1. The microorganism must be found in every case of the disease, existing in a relationship with the damaged tissue of the patient in a way that explains that damage.

2. The microorganism must be grown in a pure culture outside the patient.

3. This culture must be able to produce in healthy animals an illness which is identical in all respects to the original disease.

4. The microorganism must then be recovered from the infected animals.

Koch rigorously applied these postulates to his own research and they have since become the standards for determining the cause of any infectious disease. However, they also show how difficult it is to determine the precise cause of a disease.

turned to the study of tuberculosis. In 1882, he became the first scientist to identify the bacterium that causes tuberculosis. This long awaited discovery caused a sensation. Robert Koch became a household name almost immediately. Famous and, by this time, supported by the German government, he continued to search for a cure for tuberculosis. In 1889, he announced that he had found a substance that killed the bacteria and did not harm the body. This was tuberculin, made from an extract of dead tuberculosis bacteria. Unfortunately, further experiments showed that the substance did not stop the growth of the bacteria. However, other scientists discovered that if a person had an allergic reaction to tuberculin that was scratched into their skin, it meant they had been infected with tuberculosis. This formed the basis of the tuberculosis test that we use today.

Koch never succeeded in finding a cure for tuberculosis, although his work on the disease resulted in him winning the Nobel Prize in 1905. Although many scientists carried on Koch's work after his death in 1910, the cure for tuberculosis was still over thirty-five years away.

MAGIC BULLETS

Koch's discovery of the cause of tuberculosis did little to help people who were dying of the disease. There was still no effective treatment. Some people would live for many years with the disease, while others would rapidly die from it. Still others would go through a period of illness and then apparently make a complete recovery and never have symptoms again.

In the late nineteenth century, special hospitals for the treatment of tuberculosis began to appear. These places, called sanatoriums, were set up in the country or in mountainous areas. As the ancient Greek doctor Galen had observed, people with tuberculosis seemed to do better in thin and dry air, or by the seashore. Two of the most famous sanatoriums were Davos, in a mountain

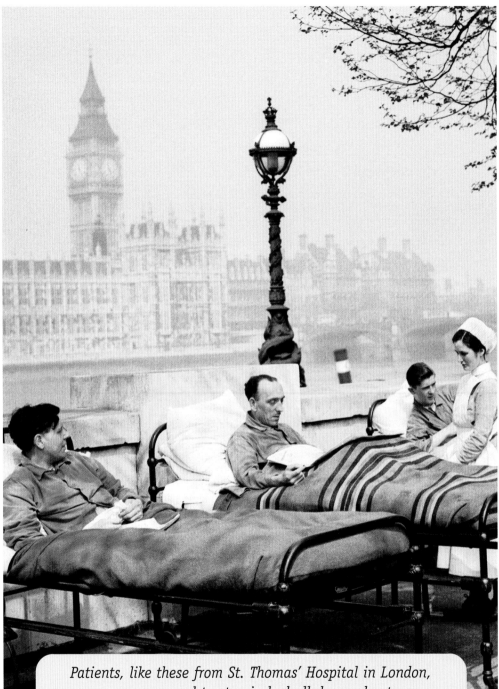

Patients, like these from St. Thomas' Hospital in London, were encouraged to stay in bed all day and get as much fresh air as possible.

valley in Switzerland—which provided the basis for Thomas Mann's famous novel *The Magic Mountain*—and Saranac Lake in New York State. Patients at the sanatoriums were encouraged to stay in bed almost the entire day. The wards were often open to the outside, to give the patients as much fresh air as possible. In some places, the belief that cold, dry air would be beneficial was taken to an almost ridiculous extreme: students were made to study outside, in the middle of winter, wearing shorts and no shirts. Patients were often served milk and raw eggs in the hope that these would help build up their strength.

For those patients with more severe cases of tuberculosis, various surgical solutions were sometimes attempted. The simplest was to remove the diseased portion of the lung. This was dangerous to the patient, not only because all surgery in this period was dangerous, but because of his or her weakened condition. Another procedure was called pneumothorax. This involved removing a rib and filling the space around the lungs with liquid or other material. This prevented the lungs from expanding to their full capacity and thus reduced the amount of oxygen they could take in. This would sometimes slow the advance of the disease, although it was painful and left the patient permanently disfigured. A third solution was to crush the phrenic nerve, which controls the action

Vaccination is when a person is inoculated with a weakened form of a disease so that he or she will become resistant to that disease without getting sick.

Inoculation is the technique of artificially infecting a person with just enough of a disease to make them sick but not enough to kill them. Once the person has recovered, he or she will then be immune to the disease. In the 1700s, the practice was introduced into Great Britain; soon, inoculation was common for those who could afford it.

Inoculation had some serious drawbacks, however. After inoculation, the patient would develop a mild case of the disease; but sometimes he or she still died from it. And during the period of the illness, the patient was highly contagious. What was needed was a method to gain the resistance inoculation brought without the risks of contagion or death. An English doctor, Edward Jenner, thought he might have a solution. Among dairy farmers it was said that people who caught cowpox—a smallpoxlike disease that affected cows but did not kill humans—could not catch smallpox. In 1796, Jenner was able to inoculate a boy with cowpox taken from a milkmaid. The boy did not become seriously ill, and later was found to be immune to smallpox. Jenner had found the magic shield against smallpox infection. He called his technique vaccination, from the Latin words meaning "taken from a cow." Jenner's discovery led to the eventual eradication of smallpox in 1977.

Later researchers, such as Louis Pasteur, discovered how to make a weakened form of a deadly virus and use it to inoculate people. Such techniques were used to create a tuberculosis vaccine known as BCG. This vaccine has been used in many parts of the world with some success; however, it has not been widely used in the United States.

of the diaphragm, the sheet of muscle under the lungs that makes the lungs expand and contract. This, too, limited the patient's intake of oxygen and slowed the growth of the disease. While all these techniques had some limited value, none of them were very effective in helping people with advanced cases of tuberculosis.

Albert Calmette, a French bacteriologist, created the tuberculosis vaccine BCG with Camille Guérin.

What was needed was a method of killing the bacteria without harming the patient. Yet for many years, little research was done in this area. This was because many scientists, observing the success of the vaccines produced in the nineteenth century, felt that the best method of combating any disease was to create a vaccine for it so that people could not catch it. Indeed, two French scientists, Albert Calmette and Camille Guérin, had created a weakened form of the tuberculosis bacteria called BCG that could be used to create a vaccine. However, there had been problems with the vaccine;

GERHARD DOMAGK

Born 1895 in Germany, Domagk was a medical student at the beginning of World War I. He fought in the German army and later became a battlefield surgeon. After the war, he dedicated his life to fighting the infections that had killed so many soldiers during the war. In 1933, his creation Prontosil became the first antibiotic drug to be widely used, and paved the way for even more effective drugs. He was awarded the Nobel Prize in 1939, but the Nazi government of Germany would not allow him to travel to Sweden to accept it.

During World War II, he discovered the first effective treatment for gas gangrene, a common and deadly infection of battlefield wounds. After the war, he created the tuberculosis-fighting antibiotic Conteben, and helped research even more powerful antibiotics. He died in 1964.

SELMAN WAKSMAN

Born in Russia in 1888, Waksman was fascinated by the microbes that live in soil. Emigrating to America in 1910, he earned his Ph.D. and eventually became a professor at Rutgers University in New Jersey. Realizing that microbes in the soil might possess the ability to kill the tuberculosis bacteria, he began a long search for such an organism. His work finally paid off with the discovery of streptomycin in 1943. Although not a medical doctor, Waksman saved many more lives with his research on the soil than any tuberculosis doctor before him. He was awarded the Nobel Prize in 1952. Waksman died in 1973.

(Continued on page 44)

JORGEN LEHMANN

Born 1898 in Denmark, Lehmann was a brilliant biologist and doctor. In 1938 he became the chief of chemical pathology in Gothenberg, Sweden. An article by an American friend gave him the intuition that the aspirin molecule could be manipulated to create a drug that could combat tuberculosis. But wartime conditions in Sweden and the difficulty in efficiently creating the drug, called PAS, prevented its widespread introduction until 1947. PAS, was not as effective as streptomycin, but without it, the triple-drug therapy that was the only effective cure for tuberculosis would have been impossible. Lehmann died in 1989.

because of bad quality control, samples of it used to combat a tuberculosis epidemic in Germany actually spread the disease. Also, some scientists and public health officials, especially in America, did not think the vaccine was effective enough. Because of this, and the difficulties in producing vaccines for other common bacterial infections, attention began to turn toward creating drug therapies. The problem was to find a way to kill only the disease-causing bacteria and not the other cells of the body; what was needed was a "magic bullet" that could cure the patient without harming him or her.

In 1933, Gerhard Domagk, a German doctor working for Bayer Laboratories, and his chemist colleague,

Josef Klarer, created a new drug called Prontosil. Although it did not affect tuberculosis, Prontosil cured many infections, such as blood poisoning, that had previously been impossible to treat. Soon, other researchers had broken down the chemical structure of Prontosil and produced even more effective drugs, called sulfa drugs, based on it.

Prontosil was an entirely artificial creation, created in a chemist's lab. Other researchers, however, were examining the natural world for clues as to how to kill bacteria. Five years before the creation of Prontosil, in 1928, one vital discovery had already been made. Alexander Fleming, a Scottish doctor, found that in bacterial cultures that became contaminated with a common bread mold, the bacteria in the cultures died wherever it came in contact with the mold. This mold, *Penicillium notatum*, produced a substance that came to be known as penicillin, one of the most effective antibacterial drugs known to humankind. Unfortunately, problems in mass-producing penicillin prevented it from making a real impact on the world of medicine until the 1940s.

However, the discovery that one naturally occurring antibiotic existed prompted many researchers to look for others. At Rutgers University in New Jersey, Dr. Selman Waksman, perhaps the most brilliant microbiologist of his day, began a long series of

In 1928, a Scottish doctor named Alexander Fleming discovered that Penicillium notatum, *a common bread mold, is an effective antibacterial agent.*

experiments to find an organism that could kill the tuberculosis bacteria. A specialist in the area of soil microbiology, Waksman was particularly suited for this task because tuberculosis lives in the soil. However, since it is not found everywhere, he theorized that there must be some other organism capable of killing it. It would take decades of research, however, to find this organism.

In 1943, one of Waksman's research assistants, Albert Schatz, found that a strange organism, not quite a fungus nor a bacteria, produced a substance that definitely killed the tuberculosis bacteria. The discovery of this substance, streptomycin, was a breakthrough in antibiotic technology and the war against tuberculosis.

Early tests of streptomycin were spectacular. Patients with advanced forms of the disease almost immediately began to improve. They rapidly gained back weight, their cough disappeared, and their lungs began to heal. Patients who had been completely bedridden were suddenly walking around again. Streptomycin was a medical miracle.

By the time that streptomycin was being introduced, two other tuberculosis-fighting drugs had also been discovered. One was Conteben, created by Gerhard Domagk by manipulating the original Prontosil molecules into a new configuration that killed tuberculosis. The other was PAS, or para-amino salt, a modification of the common aspirin molecule that was discovered by the Swedish doctor Jorgen Lehmann. Both Conteben and PAS proved to be effective against tuberculosis, although neither was as powerful as streptomycin.

It was fortunate that all three were discovered so close together. For it soon became apparent that one anti-tuberculosis drug was not enough to completely defeat this stubborn disease.

For one thing, some people had allergies to one or another of the drugs, which made it impossible for them to take it. But more ominously, doctors were

George Orwell was the pen name of the English writer Eric Blair, author of the novels *1984* and *Animal Farm*.

Orwell began to display symptoms of tuberculosis in 1938, although initial tests for it were negative. He continued to suffer ill health for several years. In 1947, during an extremely cold winter, he finally was diagnosed with tuberculosis and was admitted to a hospital. He was treated with the new drug, streptomycin. But he soon developed strange reactions to it. His skin turned red and itchy. Blisters blossomed across

George Orwell

his lips, cheeks and throat. His hair and nails fell out. After fifty days, the doctors were forced to take him off of streptomycin. However, his tuberculosis was much improved, and he was soon back at work on *1984*.

Soon, though, the strain of completing the book resulted in a relapse. Streptomycin no longer had any effect on his disease, and he died on January 22, 1950.

Today we know that Orwell had an allergy to streptomycin, which kept the doctors from completing his treatment the first time. However, even without an allergy to the antibiotic, streptomycin would not have saved his life during his second treatment, for his infection had become resistant to the drug. Orwell was one of many patients who relapsed after an initial cure. Cases like his soon pointed out the necessity of using multiple drugs to treat the disease.

finding that often one drug was not enough for any-one. There were disturbing reports that people who had been cured using streptomycin were having relapses of tuberculosis. Analysis of the bacteria in their body revealed a chilling fact: not only were they still infected, but the bacteria was no longer affected by streptomycin.

What had happened was simple enough to explain. A person who has been infected with tuberculosis will have millions of bacteria in his or her body. The vast majority of these will be killed by streptomycin or one of the other drugs. However, a very small number of these bacteria mutate or change and become immune to one or another of the drugs. If only one drug is introduced into the patient, it will kill most of the bacteria. However, the immune bacteria will survive and continue to multiply. Eventually, the patient will become ill again, but this time his or her body will contain only bacteria that are resistant to the drug with which he or she has been treated.

Soon, however, doctors discovered that if they gave the patient three different drugs at the same time, they could cure the disease entirely. This is because even bacteria that are immune to one drug are likely not to be immune to the other two drugs. Thus, by using three drugs at the same time, the person's infection could be completely wiped out.

Soon, new drugs were produced that were even more powerful than streptomycin. Tuberculosis death rates began to plummet. What had been the leading cause of death in humans for centuries vanished in the course of mere decades. So complete was this turnaround that the American Tuberculosis Society decided to change its focus to other diseases and became the American Lung Society. Infection with tuberculosis, once the stuff of nightmares, now seemed almost quaint, something out of an old book; even if someone got sick, he or she could be safely and easily cured.

But the Captain of Death was not so easily defeated. After decades of retreat, it suddenly exploded into the news again in the last decade of the twentieth century.

A NEW THREAT

For over three decades, the number of new tuberculosis cases in the United States had been falling steadily each year. In 1986, however, the number actually increased and continued to increase each year until 1993. While the number of cases never approached the epidemic proportions of the years before the introduction of streptomycin, this increase was obviously troubling to many doctors. Worse, many of the new patients had strains of the disease that were immune to several of the antibiotics. What had happened?

One reason for the increase in the number of tuberculosis cases is that in many parts of the world, tuberculosis is still a major threat. When people from these regions immigrate into new areas like the United States, they sometimes carry the disease with them, and then spread it.

A second cause is the failure of people with the disease to take all of their medicine. To be effective, the antibiotics must be taken for a period of many weeks. However, some patients, feeling better almost immediately, do not take the medicine long enough. As a result, strains of bacteria that are resistant to one or more of the drugs eventually reinfect them. Worse, they can then spread these resistant strains to other people.

The worst factor involved in the return of tuberculosis, however, is AIDS, a disease that destroys the body's natural immune system. A person who has AIDS dies not from the virus, but from the infections that attack his or her weakened defenses.

Like tuberculosis, AIDS usually takes several years to kill a person who is infected with it. Often, symptoms will not be apparent for many years. However, a person infected with both AIDS and tuberculosis can die very rapidly. The two diseases seem to mutually support each other, each one making the other work faster and more viciously. Even worse, people who have tuberculosis and AIDS often develop strains of tuberculosis that are resistant to drugs. This is because their natural defenses have been so weakened by AIDS that even with the help of antibiotics,

The AIDS Memorial Quilt commemorates the lives of people who have died of AIDS. The spread of AIDS has led to a resurgence in tuberculosis deaths.

their bodies cannot kill all the tuberculosis bacteria, allowing the resistant strains to grow even faster than they would normally.

The emergence of these multiple drug resistant (MDR) strains of tuberculosis is a serious threat to the public health of every country in the world. One strain, called Strain W, is resistant to four of the major tuberculosis drugs. It first appeared in a New York City hospital in 1990 and has rapidly spread across the United States. The tuberculosis epidemic that hit New York City in the early 1990s included many cases caused by this particularly dangerous kind of bacteria.

The discovery of effective treatments for tuberculosis in the middle of the twentieth century was one of the greatest triumphs in the history of medical science. Mankind's deadliest foe had apparently been conquered and would no longer trouble the world—or so it seemed. Looking back now, we can see that this overconfident attitude has caused people to neglect tuberculosis, and the consequences have been dire. As AIDS ravages many parts of the world, its partner, tuberculosis, is likely to re-emerge as one of the leading causes of death in the world. New antibiotics and other therapies need to be developed, or the Captain of Death may yet have the final word in its long battle with humankind.

GLOSSARY

antibiotic A drug that kills bacteria. Antibiotics have no effect on viruses.

bacteria Microscopic organisms that infect living hosts and grow inside of them.

epidemic An outbreak of a disease that infects many or most people in a certain area, such as a city or country.

immune system The body's natural defenses against disease.

inoculation Introducing a disease artificially into a person so that they become resistant to that disease.

resistance The ability of a person to successfully fight off a disease. With many diseases, if a person has had the disease once, he or she cannot catch it again.

resistant bacteria   Bacteria that have become immune to one or more antibiotics.

vaccination   Inoculating a person with a weakened form of a disease so that he or she will become resistant to the disease without either getting sick or infecting others.

virus   Microscopic parasites, much smaller than bacteria. They are not "alive" and can only reproduce within a living cell.

FOR MORE INFORMATION

In the United States

American Lung Association
1740 Broadway
New York, NY 10019
(212) 315-8700
Web site: http://www.lungusa.org

American Medical Association (AMA)
515 North State Street
Chicago, IL 60610
(312) 464-5000
Web site: http://www.ama-assn.org

The Centers for Disease Control and Prevention (CDC)
1600 Clifton Road
Atlanta, GA 30333

(800) 311-3435 or (404) 639-3311
Web site: http://www.cdc.gov

National Foundation for Infectious Diseases
4733 Bethesda Avenue, Suite 750
Bethesda, MD 20814
(301) 656-0003
Web site: http://www.nfid.org

National Institute of Allergy and Infectious Diseases
NIAID Office of Communications & Public Liaison
31 Center Drive MSC 2520
Building 31, Room 7A-50
Bethesda, MD 20892-2520
(301) 496-1884
Web site: http://www.niaid.nih.gov

National Science Foundation
4201 Wilson Boulevard
Arlington, VA 22230
(703) 292-5111
Web site: http://www.nsf.gov

The World Health Organization (WHO)
Pan American Health Organization
525 Twenty-third Street, NW
Washington, DC 20037

(202) 974-3000
Web site: http://www.paho.org

In Canada

Canadian Lung Association
3 Raymond Street, Suite 300
Ottawa, ON K1R 1A3
(613) 569-6411
Web site: http://www.lung.ca

Clinical Trial Research Center
Dalhousie University
Department of Pediatrics
Halifax, NS B3H 3J5
(902) 428–8992
Web site: http://www.dal.ca/~ctrc

Health Canada
A.L. 0904A
Ottawa, ON K1A 0K9
(613) 957-2991
Web site: http://www.hc-sc.gc.ca

FOR FURTHER READING

Daniel, Thomas M. *Captain of Death: The Story of Tuberculosis*. Rochester, NY: University of Rochester Press, 1997.

Farrell, Jeanette. *Invisible Enemies: Stories of Infectious Disease*. New York: Farrar, Straus & Giroux, Inc., 1998.

Hyde, Margaret O. *Know About Tuberculosis*. New York: Walker Publishing Co., 1994.

Karlen, Arno. *Man and Microbes: Disease and Plagues in History and Modern Times*. New York: The Putnam Publishing Group, 1995.

Landau, Elaine. *Tuberculosis*. New York: Franklin Watts, Inc., 1995.

McNeill, William H. *Plagues and Peoples*. New York: Peter Smith Publisher, Inc., 1992.

Ryan, Frank. *Forgotten Plague: How the Battle Against Tuberculosis Was Won and Lost*. New York: Little, Brown & Company, 1994.

INDEX

CREDITS

About the Author

Fred Ramen is a writer and computer programmer who lives in New York City. He is also the author of *Hermann Göring* for the Rosen Publishing Group. Fred's interests include the American Civil War, science fiction, Aikido, and the New York Mets. He was a semi-finalist in the 1997 *Jeopardy!* Tournament of Champions.

Photo Credits

Photo Library/Photo Researchers; pp. 30, 38 © Hulton/Archive Photos; p. 33 © Garry McMichael/Photo Source Inc./Photo Researchers; p. 40 © Archive Photos; p. 46 © Andrew McClenaghan/Science Photo Library/Photo Researchers; p. 48 © The Everett Collection.

Design and Layout

Evelyn Horovicz